Being
Black and
Republican in
the Age of
Obama

A Psychographic Study of Black Conservatives

Images: Shelly Duignan
Printed in the United States of America, Hill Printing
ISBN 9 781624 073144

2

I dedicate this book to my mother, "the smartest woman I have ever known," and I thank her for allowing me the freedom to think for myself and come to my own conclusions.

Lord grant me the serenity to accept the things I cannot change, the courage to change the things I can and the wisdom to know the difference.

- *Anonymous (the serenity prayer)*

F O R W A R D

As a black woman, I am often mistaken for a lot of things and being a Democrat is one of them. I guess I didn't get the memo that I can't be both black and a Republican.

So I began the journey of going through my own self-discovery. After over 2,000 hours of conducting surveys, reading census reports and other voluminous and very dry material, meeting with other black conservatives in weekly small focus groups, and of course just living my own personal story, from all that, this book was born.

To respect the privacy of those who participated in my focus groups, names were changed.

This is not an attempt on my part to proselytize for the Republican Party or to demonize the Democratic Party; instead, to begin again with an honest debate and to mend the divide which has been too costly for too many.

What the readers are saying ...

*I found this book to be a written confirmation
of my own personal experience as a black
person living in the United States today. I
consumed the entire book on a flight to
Georgia, and upon landing, it were as if I was
touching down on a new era in my political
being.*

*With every new page, a head nod. With every
new chapter, a chuckle. As I read, I found
myself pondering my own political conversion
from a loyal Democrat to a ballot-conscious
Conservative.*

~ Vincent L. Harris

A smart, savvy dose of reality—a refreshing and informative view that deserves far more attention. It is an easy but important read for all who want to understand more about racial issues, discrimination against black Republicans, and why the Republican Party should include far more blacks.

~ Sidney Powell
Author of Licensed to Lie

ACKNOWLEDGEMENT

I have said countless times that I have so few friends because all I talk about is religion and politics, but the friends I have are the best there are.

I owe a very special thanks to my dear patient and tolerant family. My amazing mother, and my wonderful siblings. Marian (sissy), Burt, and Andrew, who have always known that I was a little strange and yet still haven't kicked me out of the family. My precious friend Carol who ordered the first 5 copies of this book and didn't ask me about my refund policy (there is none).

To my uber liberal-white-hippie friend Shelly, who I am hoping forgets to vote this election but yet helped so much in the filming and recording of the weekly focus groups; to my friend Brenda who has been such a support; to my kind friend Larry for his technical support; to my new BFF Michele who suggested I write this book; to my friend Jeanne who when I told her I was writing this book, said that it sounded like a good idea and encouraged me to continue.

I also cannot fail to acknowledge and thank those brave and independent thinking black Americans who have refused to be manipulated and have stood firmly for what they believe to be right. Many were viciously attacked and called names by the "Left" just because they refused to be labeled a Democrat even though they might be ostracized by the black community.

And to so many of you who deeply care about this great nation *of ours, I sincerely thank you for your prayers and for your willingness to participate in the debate.*

TABLE OF CONTENTS

Introduction

The Republican Party began as a coalition of anti-slavery Conscience Whigs and Free Soil Democrats opposed to the Kansas-Nebraska Act submitted to Congress by Stephen Douglas in January 1854.

The Act opened the territories of Kansas and Nebraska to slavery and future admission as slave states, thus implicitly repealing the prohibition on slavery into the new territories as was designated in the Missouri Compromise.

This change was viewed by Free-Soil and Abolitionists as an aggressive, expansionist maneuver by the slave-owning South.

In the North, the old Whig party was almost defunct. They joined with others who were intensely motivated against the Act and began forming a new Party -- the Republican Party.

On November 6, 1860 Abraham Lincoln became the first elected Republican President, and on January 1, 1863 he issued by executive order the Emancipation Proclamation freeing the slaves.

One

Black Republicans didn't give up their
"Black card"

Being black and Republican is not
an oxymoron, and black Republicans
are not trying to escape their blackness.
"I love being black" said Joan a college
educated, middle aged woman who is a
small business owner. "I am proud of my
history and know my history extremely
well – studying black history led
me to become conservative."

The assumption that black
Republicans are not deeply concerned

about the black community is not only false but is almost completely opposite of the truth.

The Uncle Tom label is not only insulting but absurd. Black Republicans aren't trying to be white, they are just trying to be honest with their core values and their core beliefs.

When I asked the small group participants, many of whom are active in their church and local civic organizations about the "Uncle Tom" or "sell-out" labels they consistently shrugged it off as being a ridiculous label used to divide black people from each other and to keep blacks from talking about real issues concerning the black community. "Those that say that, don't know their history," said James an attorney for a large international firm. "But don't those labels hurt you? I asked him, "they do," he said.

An "Uncle Tom" is a vile term used to describe a black person that would take advantage of another black person for their own personal gain and would harm black people because of their own sense of self hatred. Ergo, it is a label used to connote a total untrustworthiness to the broader black community.

The "Uncle Tom" label is disproportionately and incorrectly used on black conservatives as an attempt to not only divide and ostracize them from the greater black population but to also silence their beliefs en toto. "When I tell my black friends that I am a Republican they never ask me why, they just get upset and shut down the conversation. Just talking about it upsets them" said James.

Black Republicans are rebutted almost exclusively by ad hominem attacks by both black and non-black liberals. They are rarely attacked regarding their beliefs about policies or the role or size of government.

They are quickly portrayed as traitors to their "race" and as such their opinions have no value.

The uniqueness of black Republicans is that they are not in an audience to race-bait and or use the black community for race politics or for personal financial gain or fame. Black Republicans are usually not given access to the larger black audience via the black church, black civic organizations such as the NAACP, nor black radio.

"The biggest "Uncle Toms" and "sell-outs" I know are in the Democratic Party and they are the so-called black leaders," loudly said, Bob a veteran and retired postal worker. "We [black Republicans] have no personal agenda that is advanced by being Republican," said Joan. "It is usually just the opposite. It very often is a high price to pay."

When I made the outreach to get participants together for the small focus groups that met weekly, there were many who voiced their concerns about what would happen if the word got out that they were Republican and because of that many refused to openly participate. "Do you think this will hurt my business?" one young black conservative in his early 30's asked me. It was a stinging question: I could not assure answer him that it would not negatively impact his business.

It is as if black Republicans are living their lives in the closet.

The problem with exit polls

How does one know how black people vote? The answer: Exit Polls. Especially in a general election. Exit Polls are exactly as their name describes, they are the polls taken as people exit the poll because unlike many things in today's world, your vote is a very private matter.

Exit polls indicated that in the 2008 general election 95 percent of blacks voted for Barack Obama.

But my research proves that black Americans are closeted about not
voting for the Democratic ticket and may not be answering truthfully at exit polls in such a public forum, especially when Barack Obama was at the top of the ticket. Not wanting to answer the question of "what kind of black person doesn't vote for a black president" and not wanting to debate the labels of "Uncle Toms", "sell-out", et al, would lead some to be less than honest about their vote.

There is also a much higher concentration of black Republicans in active military which is a sector that is not questioned in exit polls.

Do I believe that the overwhelming black vote went to Barack Obama?

Yes, I do.

But, I think there needs to be some adjustment to the numbers. Based on my research, I have very strong doubts that 95 percent of blacks that voted cast their vote for Barack Obama in 2008.

And here is why:

In 2010, of the 435 US House seats that were up for election, 233 had a Democratic incumbent and 32 House seats were contested by black Republicans.

How can these two worlds exist in the same universe?

That was the largest group of black Republican candidates since reconstruction. Many were new to the political scene. Two had successful bids, Tim Scott for South Carolina's 1st Congressional district who won with 65.4 percent of the vote and Allen West who won Florida's 22nd congressional district from Democratic incumbent Ron Klein with 54.4 percent of the vote.

In spite of the media (with help from Nancy Pelosi) labeling the Tea-Party as a racist organization, both Scott and West had strong Tea-Party support.

This new crop of black political candidates was very organic in that there was not a concerted effort by the Republican Party to recruit black candidates for the 2010 mid-term election. On the contrary, their support was strongly grassroots. Allen West was the only candidate of this crop who received active financial and political help from the national Republican Party.

The number of black Republican 2010 mid-term candidates is not indicative of a community that voted 95 percent for Barack Obama just 2 years earlier. Most of these candidates did not have some dramatic conversion from liberalism to conservatism in less than two short years: most of them have been conservatives for a long time. And a run for a US House seat takes a lot of planning and an enormous personal commitment of time and personal finances. Campaigns are also very taxing on the families of the candidates and hence many candidates do not enter lightly into the election arena.

The 2012 election has also seen record numbers of black Republicans throwing their hats into the ring to be candidates, so the trend continues.

Two

Blacks Republicans bleed redder than white
Republicans

There is a term that is often used
by conservatives to describe moderate
to liberal Republicans: they call them
RINOS (Republican in name only).

That term usually doesn't apply to
elected black Republicans. My research
has discovered that the moderate black
Republican is almost non-existent, partly
because of the battles fought for self
identifying as a Republican. One need
not look further than the voting record of
Justice Clarence Thomas. Justice
Thomas is one of the most

dependable conservative voices on the bench. Justice Thomas has a lifetime appointment and has no need to pander to any base or any political cycle. His conservative record stems from his core values.

"But I know that the vote of 9 out of 10 black Americans for the Democratic Party or for the leftist kinds of policies just is not reflective of their opinions"
-- Judge Clarence Thomas

Evidence can also be found in the strong Tea-Party support that the organic 2010 black Republican candidates received. The Tea-Party coined the term "RINO" and is highly opposed to moderate – to- liberal

Republicans. Herman Cain who ran for the Republican presidential nomination for the 2012 election also had strong Tea-Party support because he was not viewed as a moderate or liberal conservative.

It can be dangerous to be a black Republican

Michael Steele, the RNC chair from 2009 – 2011, was reportedly pelted with Oreo cookies at a Maryland gubernatorial debate in 2002. Anthony Miller a black Republican who was chairman of the Arizona Legislative District 20, resigned in 2011 saying that he received threats and feared for his life. Miller has also been quoted, as saying that when he was a member of John McCain's 2008 presidential campaign he was called "McCain's boy". Miller said, "I love the Republican Party but I don't want to take a bullet for anyone."

Mia Love, a very elegant and beautiful black woman who is the Republican mayor of Saratoga Springs, Utah and a 2012 Utah congressional candidate. Her Wikipedia page was vandalized the night after her speech at the 2012 RNC convention in which she declared her support for Mitt Romney as the Republican presidential nominee.

One section of her Wikipedia page called her a "dirty, worthless whore," another section called her a "sell-out" to the "right wing hate machine" and accused her of being exploited "like the House Nigger she truly is".

In the summer of 2012, while on the re-election campaign circuit, Vice President Joe Biden told an audience with a significant amount of blacks in attendance that the Republican party will "put y'all back in chains".

Debbie Wasserman Schultz, US Representative for Florida's 20th congressional district and Chair of the Democratic National Committee proclaimed that the Democratic Party is the "natural home for black Americans."

Clay Aiken of *American Idol* fame who apparently was watching the 2012 RNC convention tweeted "Playing drinking game with my brother now. We drink every time we see a black person on screen at the RNC convention. #soberasamormon"

Unlike the phantom verbal attacks and racial slurs that Nancy Pelosi said she heard from the Tea-Party rallies, the attacks against black Republicans usually are not covered by the mainstream media.

There were no outcrys of shame from the so-called women's groups for the slander of Mia Love nor the NAACP or any other well known civil rights organizations over such hateful speech.

So of course black Republicans feel vulnerable, moderate Republicans could not bear the weight of this vitriolic banter, the attacks and threats; ergo the safer identity would be as a Democrat or as an Independent.

Three

The lack of civility of the civil rights groups

While conducting my research I had 40 self professed black republican participants. Not a single one was active in the NAACP, the oldest civil rights organization in America. Though many had been previous members, all had dropped their membership. When asked why they were no longer members, almost unanimously they said that the NAACP was too political and too liberal and not only did not share their values but offended their values.

The rudeness of the NAACP to conservative voices was obvious when Mitt Romney was audibly booed while speaking at the annual meeting of the NAACP when he told the crowd that he would eliminate Obama-care to curb government spending.

This was also the same annual meeting that President Obama decided not to attend.

None of the participants of the focus group were surprised by this lack of civility.

The NAACP claims to be non-partisan but reality begs to differ. When the NAACP released their first Annual Report Card for the first session of the 112th Congress they gave every Republican member of the United States Congress and United States Senate a resounding "F."

Not a single Democratic member of the House or Senate received such a grade.

Soon after President Obama said he supported same-sex marriage the NAACP leadership endorsed same sex marriage without an open debate from its members. How could this be the urgent agenda item of the NAACP with black unemployment north of 14 percent?

The NAACP non-political?

Clearly not.

But how did this happen?

The NAACP was founded February 12, 1909 to commemorate Abraham Lincoln's 100th birthday in response to a two day riot that happened six months earlier. There were five thousand spectators that gathered in Springfield, Illinois, the hometown of Abraham Lincoln, to witness the lynching of two black men falsely accused of rape. Mobs burned down black-owned businesses and buildings and two thousand blacks fled the city.

The founders of the NAACP were an interracial group of men and women who met in New York City. They originally called themselves the National Negro Committee and later changed the name to the National Association for the Advancement of Color People (NAACP). Their first major protest came in 1915 when they protested the blockbuster film *Birth of a Nation*, which glorified the despicable Ku Klux Klan and portrayed blacks in offensive stereotypes. The film was being enthusiastically screened at the White House by Democratic President Woodrow Wilson.

And yet the NAACP's website describes their founders as a "group of white liberals that included Mary White Ovington and Oswald Garrison."

What?

White liberals?

Where did they get that?

Mary White Ovington became involved in civil rights after hearing the great Frederick Douglass a Republican, abolitionist and former slave speak at a church in Brooklyn in 1890. Oswald Garrison Villard who worked to organize a third ticket in 1900 to challenge William Jennings Bryan and William McKinley should be described as an Independent at best.

To call them liberals is to go beyond the scope of being disingenuous and must be declared revisionist history.

But why?

I suggest that the unique paradox of the black community and the Democratic Party is that the vast majority of blacks are socially conservative.

According to the Sacramento Bee: "...an overwhelming number – 70 percent – of black voters in California ... voted for Proposition 8 and helped secure its passage, according to exit polling conducted by Media Research and Mitofsky International. Latinos were 18 percent of California's voters, and through sheer numbers also contributed to Proposition 8's success. But 53 percent of Latino voters supported the measure, a much lower percentage than black voters; among white and Asian voters, 49 percent voted for the measure." Blacks are also highly conservative in matters of abortion, school choice and illegal immigration.

Blacks have also seen the underbelly and over-promised, under-delivered promises of government entitlements and most of black wealth comes from self employment and therefore many are fiscally conservative as well. Of the 40 participants in my focus group, 80 percent were entrepreneurs.

So how does a community that is socially and somewhat fiscally conservative continue to vote against its grain?

Janet, a middle aged professional and one of the focus group participants, claimed that if you tell "the black community that the Republican Party is racist then there is no need for further discussion."

I agree with Janet. Hence you have Joe Biden's "y'all back in chains" comment and therefore there is no need to have a further discussion about size, scope and role of government or taxation policies if the other party is inherently racist.

If you revise history and make all the non-blacks who participated in the civil rights struggle or were the founders of the NAACP "white liberals" then it adds to the narrative that the Republican Party is racist, and on that basis alone, the Party becomes unacceptable.

In speaking about the NAACP, Phyllis Myers, executive director of the Center for New Black Leadership states, "This is a group that, because of its politics, has become far removed from its constituents. It survives through teachers unions, labor unions. ... They allow themselves to be the sole subsidiary of the Democratic Party, and it has done a great disservice to black voters. It makes us politically impotent".

The NAACP, which has an annual budget of $27,624,433 and will not disclose its donor list, continues to run counter to the black community ideologically. They can afford to do this because of their federal and private funding.

I propose that the NAACP should change its acronym to NAADP for the National Association for the Advancement of the Democratic Party, and rightly so should lose its tax exempt status.

And what better organization to carry and affirm such a message to the black community than the NAACP.

But the Left should be careful of their alliance with the NAACP as its relevance in the black community is waning. Jonetta Rose Barras of W.E.A.L.L.B.E. stated "In its heyday the NAACP was a bulwark against racism: It protected African Americans and demanded economic equity. It deserves praise for helping alter American society. But its mission and method have become obsolete. The NAACP is like a favorite elderly relative, telling the same story every time he sees you."

In opposition to the NAACP's gay marriage resolution, Reverend Keith Ratliff who was the NAACP state conference president of Iowa and Nebraska resigned from the national board. Reverend C.L. Bryant who was president of the Garland, Texas,

NAACP, also resigned. Bryant stated that he started to have problems with the NAACP after he declined an invitation to speak at a pro-choice rally – he resigned soon after.

In 2010 Reverend Bryant began working on a documentary called *Runaway Slave* which documents his leaving the "Democratic slave plantation". Reverend CL Bryant has become a vocal conservative and is active in the Tea-Party movement. Reverend Bryant stated, "To be anything else but a Republican in this country as a black person – you must be out of your mind. It has been the Democrats who have stood in the way of progress," Bryant added, "If you seek out what you should do for yourself, you'll find that as a black American, you'd be nuts not to be a Republican."

Recent polling suggest that 30 percent of blacks are unhappy with the Democratic party. Most black Republicans are astute in history and state that many blacks who continue to vote democratic don't realize that Abraham Lincoln was the first Republican president, that the Republican Party was the abolitionist party, that the 14th amendment to the constitution which granted full citizenship rights to blacks did not have one Democratic vote, or that president Dwight D. Eisenhower, a Republican, introduced the Civil Rights Act of 1957 which was the predecessor to the 1964 Civil Rights Act. It was the first civil rights legislation enacted by Congress since Reconstruction. It was also President Eisenhower who ordered in federal troops to protect nine black children integrating a public school following the US Supreme Court ruling in Brown vs Board of Education. The list of the role of the Republican Party in its efforts to fight slavery, Jim Crow and racism since its inception as the abolitionist party in the 1800's until today has been greatly silenced.

Unfair labeling is also used to quiet the conversation with black Republicans to the overall black community, hence the labels "sell-out" and "house-nigger" used against

Mia Love. This derogatory and offensive labeling of black Republicans has created a barrier between them and the majority black community. The conservative black voice has also been barred from the traditional black public square of black radio programs and other media. This barrier is beginning to be eroded, due in part to many blacks learning of the true Civil Rights story and also having an honest review of the detriment of a liberal agenda for the majority black community.

The overwhelming majority of the participants in my focus groups were deeply invested in the black community via their churches, black fraternity/sorority organizations and many other local nonpolitical civic organizations and have vowed to stay involved.

And then it happened ...

Hurricane Katrina

"The aftermath of Katrina will go down as one of the worst abandonments of Americans on American soil ever in US history."
— *Aaron Broussard, president Jefferson Parish on Meet the Press, NBC Sept 4, 2005.*

On September 2nd, 2005, just days after Hurricane Katrina hit New Orleans, during a live on air telethon for the victims of Katrina, rapper Kanye West went off the NBC prepared script and said, "George Bush doesn't care about black people."

On August 29, Hurricane Katrina hit New Orleans. Before Hurricane Katrina, the population of New Orleans was 70 percent black, and had the highest percentage of black people of any major American city.

The black poverty rate in New Orleans at that time was 35 percent, over 10 percentage points higher than the national black poverty rate, due in part to a third of the black New Orleanians having never finished High School. That, coupled with failing schools and high crime, was just fuel for an explosive situation. Ultimately 80 percent of New Orleans and most of the nearby parishes became flooded, and the floodwater did not recede for weeks. At least 1,836 people died as a result of Hurricane Katrina. The cost to rebuild is estimated between $96 - $125 billion and for many blacks it would further the narrative that president George W. Bush aka the Republican Party is racist. President George W. Bush says that when he heard Kanye West say, "George Bush doesn't care about black people," "it was one of the most disgusting moments in my presidency." "He called me a racist," Bush told Matt Lauer in an interview about his book *Decision Points*. "And I didn't appreciate it then. I don't appreciate it now. It's one thing to say, 'I don't appreciate the way he's handled his business.' It's another thing to say, 'This man's a racist.' I resent it, it's not true."

On February 13, 2006 a 600-page congressional summary reported, "At every level – individual, corporate, philanthropic, and governmental – society failed the victims of Hurricane Katrina. Our investigation revealed that Katrina was a national failure, an abdication of the most solemn obligation to provide for the common welfare." Among 90 separate findings in the report, both New Orleans Mayor Ray Nagin and Louisiana Governor Kathleen Blanco are to blame for unnecessary deaths and suffering because of their failure to evacuate after recognizing the gravity of the situation.

The White House was fed contradictory information from its own administration that precluded it from responding rapidly.

In response to George Bush's comments in his book *Decision Points,* Kanye West said, "we are all quick to pull a race card in America".

Not surprising to myself all (100 percent) of my focus group participants had volunteered in some capacity to help those effected by Hurricane Katrina. These are not the things that sell-outs to the black community do.

Four

Why the demonization of black conservatives?

Because without a solid majority of the black vote the Democratic party would be basically a defunct political party, losing almost all national, state, and local races.

In the state of Georgia where blacks comprise 31.0 percent of the population they were 58 percent of the 2011 Democratic primary voters, while only 37.6 percent of whites voted in that state's Democratic primary. Per the US Census, in 2011 the white population of Georgia was 63.2 percent. The

Democratic Party has been losing white voters, especially white males over the age of 45 which is the highest demographic for voter turnout.

Per the US Census those voting in 2010

Race	Age	% total eligible population registered and non registered
White Males	45 - 64	52.1
	65 -74	64.0
	75 +	63.9
Black Males	45 - 64	49.0
	65 -74	51.9
	75 +	56.9

For Hispanics the highest voting demographic was Hispanic males age 75 and over 43.4 percent of the total eligible population of Hispanic men reported to the Census that they had voted in November 2010.

The Democratic Party knows that in 2010 Republican Congressional candidates won 60 percent of the white vote. By most estimates, that was the highest proportion of white voters that the GOP has garnered in a national election since World War II. With the loss of this demographic the value of the black vote increases; ergo, the Democratic Party has to "major in the minors" to protect their viability. This dwindling ideological base encourages the rhetoric of war-mongering: race wars, class wars, and gender wars.

The Democratic party also can't attract the black community with their party platform, hence the scare tactics of race baiting and race dividing by promoting fear and continuing to play the race card at every opportunity. That was the reason the Democratic Party vigorously described the Tea-Party as racist.

In July 2010 the NAACP approved a resolution condemning racism within the Tea-Party movement and called on activist to "repudiate the racist element and activities" within the political movement. That label was beginning to stick until prominent black members of the Tea-Party stepped forward to denounce those baseless attacks and announced that they oppose President Barack Obama because of his policies not his skin color.

And then as if right out of the Democratic playbook, the black Tea-Party members were called "Oreos", "Traitors" and "Uncle Toms".

Five

So-Called-Black Leaders

The term "so-called-black leaders" is a common term in the black community because it is widely believed that they have failed to lead the black community to any meaningful place. The disappointment with the so-called-black-leaders was unanimous among the black Republican focus group participants.

The race baiting by the likes of Jesse Jackson and Al Sharpton was very bothersome to the group. When I asked the participants why, they retorted that they were opportunist. "They are nothing but poverty pimps and if there is a way to profit from it, they are in it. If they can get enough dollars or media attention then they are the first to call for a boycott or start a march; other than that, complete silence," said Joan. "They want to be treated as if they're Martin Luther King Jr, but he risked his life, they risk nothing," said James.

The so-called-black leaders are perceived to be silent on what the participants felt were the main struggling issues of the black community: of poverty, illiteracy, unwed pregnancies, violent crime, and incarceration rates. These so-called black leaders are also perceived to be political instruments of the Democratic Party.

Their main business is the business of race politics. They have built hefty nest eggs for themselves by pointing out racism, real or imagined. While they – the Jesse Jacksons and Al Sharptons of the world – have become rich, the overall black community is struggling financially. What they have not done with their national platform and access to the media is to focus on real solutions to the real problems effecting the black community.

Their lack of visible results or concrete plans greatly frustrated the participants and was noted as a major reason that ranked high from the question what made you a conservative.

Black Leaders and Barack Obama

Many have forgotten that Barack Obama did not get overwhelming support from black elected leaders during the primaries. Representative John Lewis, the veteran civil rights activist, endorsed Hillary Clinton, as did Andrew Young, former US ambassador, and US Representative Charlie Rangel of New York.

In a vulgar tirade caught on tape by Fox News, Jesse Jackson said he wanted to "cut his [Barack Obama's] nuts out" and he accused Obama of "talking down to black folks." Jackson's quotes for which he quickly apologized were picked up by a hot mic before an interview in Fox's Chicago studio.

Six

Just the Facts

"... facts are stubborn things"
— President John Adams

Another catalyst for leaving the Democratic Party and becoming a black Republican, according to my survey was the perceived lack of results of liberal programs. "If the Left had made a difference for the black community that would be one thing, but the liberal policies simply do not work," said James.

Well let's look at the facts:

Per the US Census

Unemployment

blacks	1970	10.1 percent
whites	1970	05.1 percent
blacks	2010	15.3 percent
whites	2010	07.2 percent

The numbers show that blacks still remain twice as likely to be unemployed as do their white counterparts.

Poverty Rates

blacks	1970	32.8 percent
whites	1970	07.5 percent
blacks	2010	36.0 percent
whites	2010	14.0 percent

High School Completion or Higher Rates

blacks	1970	36.1 percent
whites	1970	57.4 percent
blacks	2010	63.5 percent
whites	2010	82.0 percent

Racial Residential Segregation

Per the US 2010 Study

The average non-Hispanic white person continued to live in a neighborhood that is very different racially from those neighborhoods where the average black, Hispanic, and Asian lives. The average white person in metropolitan America lives in a neighborhood that is 75 percent white. Despite a substantial shift of minorities from cities to suburbs, these groups have often not gained access to largely white neighborhoods. For example a typical African -American lives in a neighborhood that is only 35 percent desegrated (not much different from 1940) and as much as 45 percent black.

School Segregation

Per the Civil Rights Project Report that was released in September 2012, "school segregation for black students remains very high and is increasing, most severely in the South." If the goal of the Democratic Party was betterment for the black community, than even with good intentions the facts show that they have failed. Based on their results the black community owes no allegiance to the Democratic Party.

Seven

The vote for Barack Obama

Many black Republicans voted for Barack Obama in 2008. It was easy to get caught up in the "Hope and Change" and "Yes We Can" campaign of 2008. The energy and enthusiasm of the campaign was contagious.

Colin Powell, Secretary of State under George W. Bush, stated, " ...he has met the standard of being a successful president, being an exceptional president. I think he is a transformational figure. He is a new generation coming into the world – onto the world stage, onto the American stage, and for that reason I'll be voting for Senator Barack Obama." Colin Powell wasn't the only Republican to cross the aisle and endorse Barack Obama. Bill Ruckelshaus, who served in the Nixon and Reagan administrations said, "I'm not against McCain, I'm for Obama." Christopher Buckley, son of National Review founder, William F. Buckley wrote, "Obama has in him – I think, despite his sometimes airy-fairy 'We are the people we have been waiting for' silly rhetoric – the potential to be a good, perhaps even great leader. He is, it seems clear enough, what the historical moment seems to be calling for." Larry Pressler, former Senator from South Dakota, stated, "I just got the feeling that Obama will be able to handle this financial crisis better."

Charles Mathias, former US Senator and Congressman from Maryland stated "My decision is based on the long-range needs of our country and which of these two candidates I feel is better suited to recharge America's economic health, restore its prestige abroad and inspire anew all people who cherish freedom and equality. For me, that person is Barack Obama." The list of prominent Republicans, black and white, that vocally endorsed Barack Obama goes on and on.

Arthur Davis who is black, and a former Democratic Alabama Congressman who recently became a Republican and endorsed Mitt Romney at the 2012 RNC convention stated, "I really believed if Barack Obama won the presidency, it would really change the way Americans talked to each other, it would change the way we talk about each other and it would change the way we talk about race in America."

Truth be told that was the hope for all Americans as Barack Obama started his presidency with a 69 percent approval rating in January 2009.

Eight

White Guilt

There is an element of racism that still exists in America and it is evident in both the Democratic and the Republican Party. Our history of slavery in America is not one we should ignore. Slavery and segregation were brutal and completely unjustifiable. But it is a LIE to recite to the black community or any other marginalized community that racism is bigger than their God, higher than their dreams or broader than their hopes. White guilt which leads to paternalistic and condescending views and actions toward blacks is just another form of racism and should also be eradicated.

On August 28th, 1963, in the shadows of the Lincoln Memorial, Dr. Martin Luther King, Jr. said:

I am not unmindful that some of you have come here out of great trials and tribulations. Some of you have come fresh from narrow jail cells. Some of you have come from areas where your quest for freedom left you battered by the storms of persecution and staggered by the winds of police brutality. You have been the veterans of creative suffering. Continue to work with the faith that unearned suffering is redemptive.

Go back to Mississippi, go back to Alabama, go back to South Carolina, go back to Georgia, go back to Louisiana, go back to the slums and ghettos of our northern cities, knowing that somehow this situation can and will be changed. Let us not wallow in the valley of despair.

I say to you today, my friends, so even though we face the difficulties of today and tomorrow,

I still have a dream.

It is a dream deeply rooted in the American dream. I have a dream that one day this nation will rise up and live out the true meaning of its creed: "We hold these truths to be self-evident: that all men are created equal."

I have a dream that one day on the red hills of Georgia the sons of former slaves and the sons of former slave owners will be able to sit down together at the table of brotherhood.

I have a dream that one day even the state of Mississippi, a state sweltering with the heat of injustice, sweltering with the heat of oppression, will be transformed into an oasis of freedom and justice.

I have a dream that my four little children will one day live in a nation where they will not be judged by the color of their skin but by the content of their character.

I have a dream today.

I have a dream that one day, down in Alabama, one day right there in Alabama, little black boys and black girls will be able to join hands with little white boys and white girls as sisters and brothers.

I have a dream today.

I have a dream that one day every valley shall be exalted, every hill and mountain shall be made low, the rough places will be made plain, and the crooked places will be made straight, and the glory of the Lord shall be revealed, and all flesh shall see it together. This is our hope. This is the faith that I go back to the South with. With this faith we will be able to hew out of the mountain of despair a stone of hope. With this faith we will be able to transform the jangling discords of our nation into a beautiful symphony of brotherhood. With this faith we will be able to work together, to pray together, to struggle together, to go to jail together, to stand up for freedom together, knowing that we will be free one day.

This will be the day when all of God's children will be able to sing with a new meaning, "My country, ' tis of thee, sweet land of liberty, of thee I sing. Land where my fathers died, land of the pilgrim's pride, from every mountainside, let freedom ring." And if America is to be a great nation this must become true. So let freedom ring from the prodigious hilltops of New Hampshire. Let freedom ring from the mighty mountains of New York. Let freedom ring from the heightening Alleghenies of Pennsylvania!

Let freedom ring from the snow capped Rockies of Colorado!

Let freedom ring from the curvaceous slopes of California!

But not only that; let freedom ring from Stone Mountain of Georgia!

Let freedom ring from Lookout Mountain of Tennessee!

Let freedom ring from every hill and molehill of Mississippi. From every mountainside, let freedom ring. And when this happens, when we allow freedom to ring, when we let it ring from every village and every hamlet, from every state and every city, we will be able to speed up that day when all of God's children, black men and white men, Jews and Gentiles, Protestants and Catholics, will be able to join hands and sing in the words of the old Negro spiritual,

"Free at last! Free at last!
Thank God Almighty,
we are free at last!"

Michele Bachman

Rick Santorum

John McCain

Allen West

Conclusion

It is my sincere wish that the debate can begin again, openly, honestly and fairly about which policies, programs and size of government actually have been proven to work best for the overall black community.

And that we can together begin to do the work that still awaits us.

Thank you

About the author

Karen Watson lives in Highland Park, TX with her dog Ruby. She is the founder and president of GOPBuzz.com and is already working on her next book, "How the Democrats got the black vote and How the Republicans can win it back" due out Lincoln's birthday February 12, 2014. She is available for speeches; seminars and workshops. She may be reached at:

karen.watson@gopbuzz.com

office   469-321-0076